# Heavy Weather

## Ness Lobo

# Introduction.

I remember writing my first poem when I was 12 years old, I also remember being scared of poetry and thinking, what I was writing wasn't good enough to fit in that category, so I would hide all my writings in a little box under my bed.

The feeling never left, I'm still scared of poetry, I still don't understand poetry but somehow that's what made me fall in love with it. I don't have the box anymore but I kept writing. The box became a book and the book is now in your hands for you to read, and love or hate it.

Some of these pieces were written when I was breaking with tears on my face, others were written when I was in a deep darkness, falling in love, lost, swimming in happiness or giving my heart.

This is my small journey, a part of my soul.
This is all the heavy weather in my head.

To God

and so the thunder came…

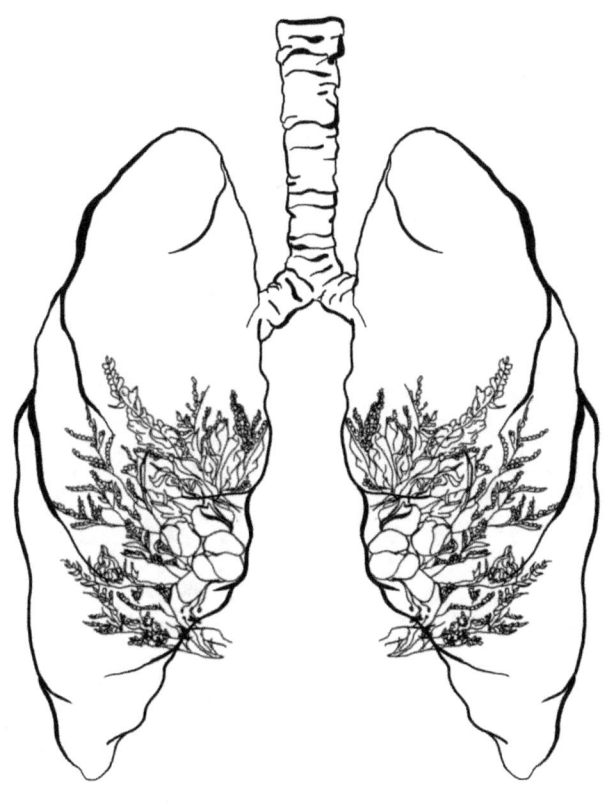

your name,
the beautiful name my heart will never forget,
the one name that makes my whole body tingle
that makes me want to go back and choose another path
before I make the mistakes I made
and end up with nightmares full of regrets.

why couldn't your name lay next to mine every night?
why did you have to run away from me when all I wanted
was to hold you close in my arms
when all I wanted was to share with you all the love I had?

and now whenever I hear your name my heart will ache,
my fingers will move touching my skin with my nails
wanting to rip off my flesh.
the voices in my head, the memories coming back in flashes, driving me insane
telling me I'll never be good enough to make you stay.

it doesn't matter what I do, it never did,
but now I'll have to live with your name on my body
like it's sealed with ink on my skin
now, I'll have to live with the pain
I'll have to live with the tears
because your name is like a red wine stain on my white dress.

and your name will remain as the one I should never forget.

—**your name.**

when you loved me
my depression didn't matter,
the ghost wouldn't haunt me.

when I thought you loved me
I felt happy.
you were giving me so little yet so much
I felt strong.

**—then I realized.**

I keep waiting for your words,
for your voice to call my name.
your soul is still present in my body
I still breathe your cologne
stuck in the air.

I want to give up.

> **—you were more than I could handle.**

you keep going back and forth
wandering around my heart
moving the furniture,
treating it like home.

unstable ocean waves,
you come and go.
your presence is the drug my veins are craving,
your substance is needed for my breathing.
I know this is bad.

you are bad.
you are bad.
you are bad.

and soon you'll be gone,
but soon you will come back to my arms.
you'll come running, rushing, begging.
We are torture.

**—second thoughts.**

my hands are shaking.
my core is crumbling down
my soul is breaking
and my whole spirit is tearing apart.

we could still be
what we said we would be,
what we wanted to become.
you can still be here.

save me.

                      **—don't leave, please.**

come and hold my soul
so maybe I could feel alive again,
maybe
I could feel my heart beating on my chest.

make my cold body
warm again.

**—missing you.**

bury me six feet under
forget about my existence,
smother me.

I am all your flaws reflected in your mirrors,
all the flaws you once loved.

**—emptiness.**

all your lies fall between
the hands and the vessels
of the broken ones,
the ones you've used,
taken and thrown
to an empty cave
and covered them in blood.

**—your careless words.**

the light bulb is flashing.
switching
on and off
on and off.

start a flash fire
burn the neighborhood.
even my house
is copying your behavior.

**—electricity.**

I am worn out
from carrying all your bags,
from hearing your voice neglect my love.

I spent all my days and nights
falling down the hole you dig for my body.

you couldn't love me
but you couldn't let me go either.

— **broken.**

lines within the tears
made up with ink,
pages and words
making love to each other
suddenly bursting apart
exploding inside their bodies.

                        **—this is what we were.**

the scars of the lovers that went wrong
are glued to my skin,
like dead bodies in their grave
not buried so deep
so that anyone can see.

the agony is taking over,
feels like I'm drowning
in an empty house
where the only visitors
are the other girls
you murdered more than once.

I'll stay here until I become
another ghost in your box.

**—last drops of you.**

my heart refuses to accept
small drops of love
falling from your bitter
breathless
soul.

—a.

how I miss the days when I could sleep
tasting those red lips,
now I'm a statue made of iron
floating in waters of anger and curses
with your ex-lover's bodies around me.
my head is drowning under the rain.

you are destruction.

—**blur.**

you were my silver lining.
my red virgin oil
was in your hands,
I thought you'd make the grass grow,
turn the oil
into a
red
burning
flame.

soon you were gone.
you lied, but I did too.

**—liars.**

it is past midnight
but our clouds are silver.
your colors have merged with mine,
we fought the rain
the storms
the thunder.

we lost.

    **—our love didn't survive our winter.**

I still have days
moments
seconds,
when I need you here
holding me tight at night
preventing my nightmares.

you were my world.

sometimes,
you still are.

**—warm hands.**

I cried tears so pure, so real
they burned my skin
when they fell off my chin.
my heart felt like it didn't belong
inside this cage.

I waited for so long
so long your absence became my lover,
your presence my enemy.

—#55.

silence can hurt you more
than a thousand bullets
encrusted into your eyes,
into your heart.

talk to me.

**—mispronounced.**

the earth was shaking,
our love was coming to an end
still I stayed.

the water was getting to my knees
our Atlantis would sink,
I forgot how to swim
you aren't here to save me.

the earthquakes pulled us down,
I thought our love was holy.

—**us.**

your love for me
was like diamond shaped mountains,
upward falling waterfalls
floating gardens and transparent castles.

it never existed.

**—nameless.**

take my sternum out of my chest
take my lungs and make them explode,
with my bones
feed the dogs.

take what's left
hide it on the coast,
in a place you know it won't be found again.

do with my body
as you did with my love.

                                                          **—hurt.**

we couldn't act like there was love in our hearts,
so we had to start a war.

**—it would have never worked.**

I found myself lost
in your darks and blues,
whites and greys.

your words
trying to change my shapes,
forcing your colors into mine.

only to fulfill the needs of the beast
hiding beneath you.

         **—silence.**

sometimes I wish
I hadn't woken up the day
we met on the second floor
where you held me
so close,
I couldn't stop myself
from falling
in love
so
innocently.

**—the day I met you.**

keep talking about her lips
how she bites them with her teeth
and how the tip of her tongue
stays outside her mouth when she smiles.

it's almost like you need her
to breathe
to live.

but you're here
with me.

**—I love you hadlich, he said.**

I knew how broken you were from the first moment
we spoke,
your last lover stabbed your trust
and you built up walls around your mind,
your beautiful mind.

I wanted to show you
how mesmerizing you are
but I could never knock them down.

       **—walls between us.**

there are oceans between us,
the distance is unbearable.
our feelings are floating on the surface
hoping to reach the border
where we stand
so far from each other.

**—we're holding hands.**

the emptiness on my chest
is drowning my soul.
the thought of you with somebody else won't leave my head
you're gone,
I'm dying in silence
trying
to forget the essence of your body.

the memories come back in fractions
lips move in slow motion
not a second of distraction,
tears fall on my face
while I hear
every piece of me
breaking.

**—I am trying.**

your mouth
telling me to glue my lips together
to stitch my eyes
so my tears would not fall.

ignoring all the words
my fingers had written with bleeding ink
hiding your name between the letters,
making me want to erase them all.

why did I ever let you hold my soul?

**—2:45am.**

maybe our love was supposed to be
as turbulent as the waters in the ocean
when a storm is hitting and thunders
are falling from the sky.

but I don't think I was supposed to drown.

**—waves.**

I heard her voice
saying your name,
I felt the confusion taking over my existence
as I fell off the bed to a never-ending hole.

memories of your face
everywhere.

          **—bottom.**

I'm tired of your lips whispering elaborated lies,
lovely words to my ears.

I want honesty,
I want love.
I want the excruciating pain of reality.
the kind of pain you feel after the love of your life
fades away.

**—you came back.**

it is the one who holds the gun
the one responsible for my bleeding.

it is him who should feel guilty,
not me.

**—it was not my fault.**

when I saw you
my soul felt like it had found the one
with an angel shape.
your holy hands made me feel safe,
made me feel warm.

then you set me on fire,
acted like you couldn't hear my screaming.

and left me there to die.

**—stop looking.**

I keep the hearts of ex-lovers I've murdered
inside a jar
under my bed.
I held yours in my hands,
caressed it.

it was not mine to hold
nor to keep.
after you left
your name written on my lungs stayed.

**—and you stole my heart.**

I saw the truth in your eyes
but your eyes could tell lies
bigger than the ones that would run in your mouth,
heavier than the ones your tongue could ever lift.

**—I named it after him, but I changed it.**

we followed the voices
when we should have been running
finding a place to stay
to save us from ourselves,
from the monsters we create.

break the silence
bring echoes into existence,
hold it to my head
and pull the trigger.

**—my darling, kill me.**

I would hold my ground
but I don't know where I stand,
your swinging love
coming back and forth
sizzling in my head
when my veins begin to boil.

start the fire,
let it burn.

**—tension.**

all the colors went dull
when the love I believed in
disappeared from my sight
and the remains of what we were,
melted when the sun came out.
all of me disintegrated,
my heart stopped beating.

**—the end.**

he wrapped me under his wings
hypnotized me with his tongue,
made of me his midnight pleasure.

his words were poems
he wrote inside my veins,
he tried to take my eyes
when I fell asleep next to him
the day we were left alone
in a room where his other lovers were killed.

      **—adventures with a fuckboy.**

pastel pink lingerie hanging in my closet,
little pink panties, little pink garter
when I'm wearing them
you will want to put me in your pocket.
your mother warned you about women like me,
women like me are forbidden.
we are the sluts you hide from your friends,
we are the sluts you judge,
yet we are the sluts you love to fuck in the dark.

pastel pink nail polish, pastel pink lip gloss
do it quick, do it fast, you can't last long.
ask me to turn off the lights,
you don't want to look me in the eye.
you can't bear with the guilt
you can't bear with the pressure,
if your mother finds out she'll cry
turn off the lights you say,
as you keep lying to yourself.

you are addicted to me,
to the tight walls between my legs
to my pastel pink smell
to my pastel pink taste,
to the touch of my pastel pink hands.

you are ashamed of who I am
you are ashamed of the shape that represents my pastel pink love.
you are ashamed of the truth I hold.

         **—pastel pink.**

don't bite your nails
release the monster.
make me cry,
ruin my weather,
call me a disgrace.

**—I don't believe you when you say you love me.**

I swore I'd love you till the end of time
but your lies burn like fire
and my soul is a ticking bomb waiting to explode.
my body sits lonely in the darkness of my empty room,
my broken lungs are getting tired of breathing
the smoky air that's filling my broken spirit
and my aching heart.

I'm fighting to survive,
my fists are hurting
you aren't holding me.

take me,
from this agony.

**—I thought I'd still love you.**

all the emotions
you put in my heart,
fell on my face
like the rain on a winter day.

**—tears.**

I hate myself
for reminding you I miss you.
you've taken away my willingness to love
to share pieces of my soul
to bathe myself in joy,
I hate myself for loving you.

**—I texted you at 2am.**

handwritten letters,
old pictures of us
floating on the surface.
all the memories and love marks
get carried away by emotions
on a river made of feelings and tears.
while I'm sitting in the dark
watching it all disappear,
our love wasn't as strong
as I thought it would be.
I sit lonely screaming in silence.
I can't cry, my eyes hurt
my tears have been crystallized.
fingers, skin, dreams
have been paralyzed under
the pressure of the words
that came out of your mouth.
still I am
looking for a phantom that is hidden
in the shadows of the love you left behind.

**—you were the one.**

I believed you when you said
I didn't have to be afraid now,
now you're in my life
now I have a knight to protect me
from the monsters at night.
you'd take care of my dreams,
watch me in my sleep.

why does it feel like you're taking my ribs
and throwing them into the fire?

**—I believed in you.**

you love to pretend you're here,
thinking you'll carry me on your shoulders
when the rain is falling
filling my house,
when the water is forcing its way
inside my furniture.

holding on to your manhood
thinking so highly of yourself.

all you are is an empty face
an empty body
an empty soul.

**—he was 27.**

I'm in love with the way
you broke my heart
dancing with me
stomping your feet on the pieces,
like it didn't matter.

I love the way
you crossed the line
and wandered in my private lawns,
like you didn't care.

I adore how we both
died stabbed in the back,
bleeding to death and we didn't mind.

**—violent love.**

your words and bullets
became my shield and can't get to my skin,
I'm stuck in your mud
but your rocks no longer break my windows.

you've taken my heart
buried it in dust.
I don't need the pills,
I'll cut through.

                      **—you destroyed me.**

you were the beast
waiting to be tamed,
don't tell me now you're scared of the cage
only because I'm in it.

—**nadie.**

can we stop pretending
we grow new hearts every day,
stop hurting each other,
start flooding our bodies with the love we desired
before we decided to use our words
as weapons and not as healing raindrops?

I'm tired of my heart aching.

> **—may 24th.**

you built a paper house for us to live in,
after a few months
the sky turned grey and the rain came.
our paper house could no longer stand.

you went running
but I stared at our house
falling down,
faster than I thought.

    **—should have loved me more.**

it's like walking in a dark forest
without clothes on,
all the trees standing tall
creating scary forms with their branches.
little lights
guiding me,
luring me to go deeper.

I can't stop my feet from moving,
the path is well marked
with four thousand white gems
that cut my feet every time
I step on them.
I am bleeding,
but I love it.

**—I knew you weren't good for me.**

you were a big
old brick wall
standing tall, rising up to the sky.

I was a guitar with three strings,
I couldn't play the chords you wanted to hear.
still,
I tried.

**—oh but I loved you.**

there's a ghost lying next to me
marking your silhouette on my bed,
your smell comes crushing
as it leaves bruises on my muscles.

tell me you love me,
give me back my ring
watch me bleed,
remind me we were a mistake.

wake me up from this nightmare,
I can't escape the mouths whispering to my ear
the hands pulling my hair.

the ghost is here to stay.

**—wash my bed sheets.**

your voice is still getting lost
in the void of the jail you call home.
in between the cells I can see your face,
your silence says a lot more words
than you ever did before.
pride is taking all over your mouth
and keeping it shut.

       **—I still think of you.**

black lines on white paper,
not drawing the iris on my eyes.

lifeless portrait,
dry lips
dead soul
red background.

your brush killed every feeling in me
with your selfish hands.

—**picture.**

you represented the idea
of the greatest love I had ever found.

it was like digging walls
promising to find a paradise on the other side.

**—illusions.**

I put all my years around me
and your finger pointed at the ones you wanted take,
my demons surrounded me
I heard them laugh
they knew we were made to wreck.

I couldn't see the truth,
and now we'll drown in the flood of our thorns.
lay our hearts on the bed
let me watch them bleed until I know yours is dead.

**—all of them.**

I will never be your cursive handwriting,
or the loving pressure you handle your pencil with.

I'm the one who cannot hold your hand in the sunlight,
the one you love when you need
to release the chained beast living under your skin.

I was not smart
when I followed your footsteps crawling
in undeniable sins
thinking you could fix my willingness to live.
my willingness to be.
my willingness to become.

—#77.

he said he needed the flames in my gaze,
in the shadows
his hand would intertwine with mine.

under our dark clouds
I fell in love with his shape
on my window pane,
his face was the highlight of my day.

slowly
I felt his hands slipping away in the rain.

—**grasp.**

you appeared to be the most beautiful symphony
whispering the right words to my ears.
you seemed to be a wonderful mystery,
everlasting puzzle
I wanted to spend my life resolving.

it is for mistakes like this
that I have swallowed my keys
to prevent new plants from growing.

**—think twice.**

can't remember the sounds,
the vibrations from the vocal cords
so soft
making my heart stop.
don't remember the spark in your eyes,
those brown beautiful eyes.

I see a thousand faces
but I can't recognize any,
none of these is yours.
all of me is aching,
the oceans flowing in my veins are boiling.

**—the last day.**

I gave you all my pieces to build me up,
to build me up like I'm a castle
lift me up.
put me high up in the clouds
and guard my doors like they were yours.

your hands took each of them
tried to change what they were.

left me standing in knives
made me feel your robbery
your laughter,
made me watch you hide all my parts.

**—innocently in love.**

I cried every time
dopamine ripped off my lungs
while I waited for my dead kiss.

I kept running,
he found poisoning plants
he put them in my mouth.

—**careful.**

your hands touched my lips,
your hair held me like I am fragility and sins.
but your teeth would hold on to the lies
of your screaming eyes under the moonlight,
during that night you killed my heartbeat.

**—red moon.**

if you were brave enough
to hold me in your arms
you would feel the universe
become dust in the blink of an eye.

but beasts are weak.

**—destruction.**

crawling away
from the moment you called my name,
escaping from the broken bones.

my eyes and heart are floating
on a sea of blood.
the rain will fall over my head,
my body will be covered in clay
and you will hang my lungs on a marble arch.

—**periit.**

I sold my soul
to the freezing depths of the sun,
under the silent waters of our loving rivers.
silver rivers longing the bleeding.

it was him
he was my sun.

## —murderer.

I threw my love all over you
to fill your empty lungs and save you from the fall,
but my hands to your eyes were invisible ghosts
trying to reach your soul.

my pearls are still your pearls
my diamonds are still your diamonds
my love still holds tight to your bones.

**—toxic.**

I want to sleep alone,
but I want to sleep alone next to you
on a bed where your body is nothing but a soul
and your soul is doing nothing but craving love.

do I have to hold your hands?
kiss your lips?
whisper your name to my pillow as I cry my heart out
every night because you don't know mine.
do I have to get a tingling feeling between my legs?
use my mouth and tongue to swirl around a private place.
do I have to say I love you every second?
every single second of the day
I love you
I love you
I love you
I love you
I love you
is that enough?
will you hold me now?
are you still here?

> **—but I wrote a poem for you.**

I'll hide your white ring
under a thick layer of snow,
a thousand miles under
where the boiling earth
meets the frozen dirt,
a place where my skin
cannot feel the burning metal
reaching to my bones,
a place where my blood isn't reminded of your name.

**—that one ring you gave me.**

once I forgot my name
his fingertips held me hostage,
all the thoughts he brought up
put me in a transparent cage.

I will vomit my heart,
watch it as it falls
from the edge my lungs are holding on to.
watch it break
watch it drowning
once it hits the crashing waves
of the ocean his love once kept calm.

         **—watch.**

all our moments
every brick that held our empire
are slipping away from my hands.
our love
burning in the dark
and the promises that once were mine
fall in fractions to the ground.
I wanted to keep your light next to me,
I thought your words were real.

**—denied the truth.**

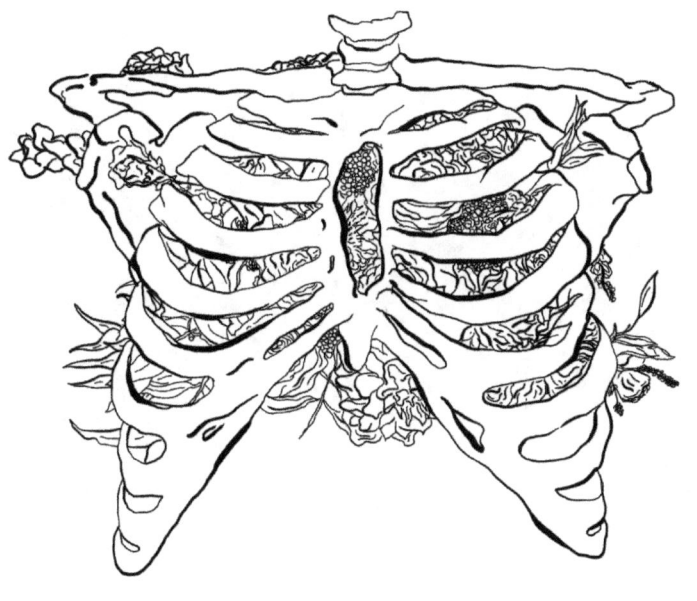

the heart that once loved you
won't return to your broken arms
to your broken soul.

it cannot stay
it cannot hold the weight of your bruises anymore.

**—the day you lost me.**

you begged for a second chance
and when it was placed in your hands
you tried to kill me,
stop me from breathing
tried to keep digging
to break me
again and again.

I was never yours to keep.
your lips and mine
we're not meant to stay together.

**—probably not the last time I'll write about you.**

I wish you had given me
more reasons to write love songs
not sad verses,
more reasons to stay
not to leave.

       **—honestly.**

put me on the front lines
sacrifice my life
for your pleasure.

leave some black roses on my grave.

**—about love.**

you've met my demons,
walked through my thoughts,
saw my pain and face
blending together.

you still wrote your lies
all over my walls.

> **—you don't understand my anxiety.**

my trust,
delicate
glass of wine,
stabbed with thorns
sharpened like knives.

you broke it down into pieces,
painted them
with your soft colored lies.

**—mortuus est dilectio.**

I wanted to love you every day
I wanted to give you my all.
stand next to you
for three thousand years' straight
love you,
until my face became a stone made of salt
and the sky ripped apart
by the white horses
galloping down carrying a black hole
ready to eat us whole.

—**funeral.**

my thoughts are now sane
my nights are quiet
my demons remain silent,

you are diving into the cave
you buried me in
when my heart was yours to keep.

hold your breath.

**—he keeps calling.**

sitting in isolation,
mirrors breaking
falling on me
cutting my skin.

I'll swallow the earth,
explode in the universe
so that maybe I can stop feeling this pain.

**—our love story.**

I will keep my heart quiet,
remove my shoes
and walk away from you.

I will remain silent.

       **—you won't notice.**

the moon is following my steps
watching me from the sky,
the night shadows
walking behind my back
carrying candles
made of tears and burning fire.

shrunken skulls
hanging from my black dress,
the ghosts have their masks on
voices sing mourning songs
while creatures play the drums
like it's a cult.

holding our beating hearts on my hands,
I will bury them in the sand.
mother night cries
our love died.

**—may 16th.**

all of me falls like dominoes
standing on a bridge.

rest your head on my chest
for the worst has been said,
you were my dream
your crystals were as clear
as the air running through your hair,
I loved you,
I loved you.

**—my achilles heel.**

when the time comes
you'll think of me.
you'll think about the spark in my eyes
my spirit and soul
jumping up and down.

you'll remember how I always wanted you
to make a wish with me,
oh how I wish you did
but you never,
never,
never looked at me.

         **—11:11.**

she used her hands like they were mine,
combed her hair
and stitch you like I did,
she put your eyelids together
using a black thread,
you couldn't see.

she wanted you to believe she was like me,
except I stitched your broken pieces.

**—stolen.**

I got caught up in your empty love traces.

the pressure of your knives and ropes
make me feel like my heart will stop beating.
you cannot break me
your lies are weak
your tears are fake
your strength is gone.

I wasted red chords and grey tones.
how I wish I could go back to avoid
finding your false gold statue lying on the floor.

                **—I thought you were a diamond.**

I hate the random butterfly
I feel on my chest
screaming your name
trying to bring you back.

desperately hunting you
like it could give you life.

—**runaway.**

I am the apple falling from the tree
on Eve's hands being offered to you.
a sin opening your eyes
giving you a sight of a new life,
getting your hopes up
only to let you kiss the ground.

I am the punishment of your heart,
the one you'll call a quitter
still you will fall in love.

I am the one you'll never forget,
the nights you spend with her
I'll be on your mind,
your days will be bitter
when you hear my name.

I am the one who will be in the dreams
you call nightmares.

and you are the man I could never fall in love with.

**—prohibited.**

the strange look in her eyes
would leave you craving.
she would paint a picture
of what could have been.

one look,
and you'd feel like you had traveled
the world by her side
her mind was tragic
but without her you'd go blind.

you needed her,
you needed her to talk about the places
you've never seen,
you needed to hear her excitement
describing the dream she had last night.

you wanted her.
you desired her.
she loved you.

—**gone.**

all the days I spent loving
I've been swimming in boiling water.
his good intentions don't exist
no matter the words he says
or how he moves his hands
or how he kisses me in the middle of the night.

my willingness to love is buried
under the spit of his lies.

         **—cold.**

I've lived the fake
disposable
deficient love.

the one love that doesn't help you carry your burdens
instead it loads your back with theirs without asking.
the kind of love that takes pride in your wounds,
doesn't' lift you up when you're feeling down.

it hates you more than it loves you,
it needs to see your bruises go darker
this love uses you,
this love hurts you.

**—so many years lost.**

my skin got thicker
when you smiled and your teeth looked like sharks
coming at me.
the storm in your mind
created chaos and I died.

the necklace you put on my neck
fell on the floor.
it was intoxicating me,
like you.

**—learn**

I want every cell in my body
to be ripped apart and filled up with anger
against you.

I can't do it
and I hate myself for it.

**—why.**

shouting my name outside my house,
your throat breaking up
your soul falling apart.

the blood in your veins is screaming
regretting when you said
my eyes wanted to steal your all
and drown it in the river of sins.
when you said,
I would turn your body
into solid stone
to match the shape of your heart.

—**accusations.**

part of me
wants to move mountains for you,
part of me
wants to wait for you to prove your words are true.

**—realizing we are over.**

the good man I've been seeing since you left
is the kind of man I know my mother would love,
this good man is the kind of man who cares
he is the kind any girl would want.

he would drive to your house
only to get you chocolate ice cream because
you're on your period and you have chocolate cravings.
this good man would save me, if I needed saving.
if I needed a hug and we were on opposite sides of the world
he would drive to the closest shore, take off his clothes, get in the water
he can't swim but that doesn't matter.
fight the sharks, look at the stars, find the place where I am
to give me that one hug.

the good man has white teeth, is sweet and has a good breath,
when I'm sick I know he will be there.
he is the kind of man I know I should marry,
but I still can't get my heart out and put it in his hands,
and not because I'm not ready
this good man is probably everything I've ever wanted and more.

I feel bad for this good man,
he is giving me all he can
but he is not you.

**—all the other guys.**

two worlds
spiraling
waiting to collide
inside our bodies,
ready to destroy our strength.

    **—what it felt like when we held hands.**

the way you loved me
was cold like a mirror,
your heart
an inhospitable palace
occupied by demons,
my face and hands could not survive
the burnings in your walls.

I tried to save you from this hell,
I couldn't.

**—antarctica.**

the feelings,
the passion
leaving my body
escaping the cages
opening the gates with burning weapons.
running away from me
like birds flee from the cold winter.

in the dark
the memories disappear
slowly erasing themselves
as my blood is emptying my veins.

I'm falling out of love.

      **—we said forever too fast.**

the floor is burning my feet
I can't touch all the wonders you hide,
I never will.
every second the clock is ticking
I am further from your arms
my stardust will leave you.

you are too consumed in your own existence
to see you're bleeding.

—**beheaded.**

the longing of your body
spiraling down the line of the ones
you once loved and then forgot.

you should have taught me
how to live
without your voice.

**—dark brown beard.**

thoughts, feelings, poems about you
stumble upon my heart.
they make me fall in love
fall out of love,
cry at night until the sun comes out.

my heart, your heart
are like oil and water
me being the water
you being the oil.

**—today I felt sorry.**

one day you'll wake up
wishing you heard my voice
calling your name,
before you broke my tongue
and locked me inside a silence castle.

**—you'll miss me.**

my feet moved away from you
before your hell would swallow me whole,
turning my bones to dust.

**—I ran away.**

your hands were hungry for revenge,
my spirit was hungry for you
wanting to lose myself
in your dark brown eyes,
holding on to the thought
of you giving life
to my body with your words.

I believed I was enough
to cease your need for blood,
I wasn't.

I had to stop my heart from racing
I had to let you go.

**—I wanted more from you.**

I am changing
as all my seizures fade away
with the sound of your gun
shooting against my lungs.

the chains that once held me
are breaking.
your violence set me free.

        **—fearful.**

my mouth pronounced forbidden words.
my eyes cried invisible empty tears
and not a part of my soul left my body.

my heart turns to stone
when his cold hands murdered my skin.

**—do you still love him? no.**

the devil is going to bless your soul,
lick every part of you
with his evil tongue.

in the name of every mouth your lips touched.

**—men.**

don't pronounce his name
don't talk about the mole
on the left side of his face
or his red shoes,
or the way his hands would move
around my body.

my eyes don't hold any water
my whole spirit is exhausted,
he kept my treasures
but he is gone,
so am I.

—**forever.**

you'll say I'm a child
turn off my night light,

your body
used to be enough to calm the monsters
stop them from stealing my peace,
but it doesn't soothe me like before.

now
I
need
the
light
more.

                                **—killed it.**

little ghosts
taking pieces of his day
throwing them into our suffocating silence.
frozen chariots that were once
made of fire,
every flame
a melting lie.

his fingertips across my room
reminders of his selfish ways.
the air I breathe is not the same,
I was meant to love you
but my heart left my chest.

**—I won't let you hurt me.**

I'm sorry

for loving you the way I did,
for going too far
giving you things you couldn't keep.

for holding on to feelings that weren't mine,
forgive me for waiting too long.

I'm sorry I didn't move,
in my dreams my heart believed
you wanted to be with me.

**—my dearest.**

every now and then
you'll watch the rain
fall in your garden,
you'll remember my face,
how I loved those flowers
and the smell of wet soil
after the storm.

                                        **—but that's it.**

I once fell for a boy pretending to be a man,
playing with the dolls he found on the road.
his selfish soul seemed to be as bright as the sun
but it was as dark as the nights
when the choir stays in silence
for there is no joy in their hearts to sing about,
their minds are filled with sorrow
they stay quiet.
he wrote his name on the wall of the manly men
he wrote it with the sweat of his forehead,
sealed it with the eyes of girls who went to testify.
blind girls who fell for his manipulative gaze.

somehow
I managed to survive.

—**falsedad.**

before we walked all the deserts
looking for drops of beating blood,
to save us
to save our soul,
you fell on quicksand
and tried to drag me in.

for you I would have stayed
instead
you made me feel guilty for leaving.

—**him.**

I once wrote about a good man,
his poem was long but I made it short.
he
was
just
a
boy.

**—part 2.**

brown,
the color of his eyes
the color of my morning coffee,
it tastes like him
it smells like him.
feels warm like his arms once did,

hold me tight
kiss my forehead.

wake me up.

**—I forgot you weren't here.**

we were made to blend
then bend and brake
like fragile porcelain.

we were a flower growing
in the midst of the desert
rising against the poison
in our heads.

we lost our strength
there was no surviving
soon we were drowning,
a small breeze took me away
and you were left on your knees
waiting for the snakes.

>                              **—we died.**

sometimes my demons regret
making me leave you,
they don't feel your hands
leaving marks on my skin.

there is no pain
there are no tears
there is no torture,
there isn't a rope choking my throat.

—**aggressive.**

when the roots are no longer bleeding,
when you find yourself swimming
in a lake of blood to find your name
written on black sand,
when you start to count the sacred thorns,
break the stones that lay inside of you

that's when you'll know I still carry you
in the deep ends of my heart
protecting you from all the hands
wanting to rip you off from the ground.

> **—but I don't love you anymore.**

we were deceased,
our limbs were infected
with the perversion of your pleasure,
I was walking with chains on my wrists.

**—I was an object to him.**

the feelings are drifting away
from the boxes in my soul.
I'm sure there is a God that will save me
from drowning.
so pull me out
throw me in again,
break my pieces with the pipes
polished with lies.
watch me
through your fire eyes,
lock me
in a room without oxygen
until I can't breathe.

**—I don't know how to forget about you.**

walking
following invisible footprints.
all our insecurities are following
our shaking bodies running
in fear of falling to our knees,
finding our old bed sheets
as we crawl in circles.

silence falls into the darkness
of our love breaking like fake stones.

**—we found each other again.**

bleeding eyes
non-beating heart.
your spirit is trapped
in a cage filled with sorrow,
wanting to scream
there is a knife stuck on your throat.
the snake is crawling up your leg,
you'll die smothered
by the excruciating pain.

it will take you home.

**—you can't hold me anymore.**

his breath was my drug,
his words were poetry and curses
infecting everything that was left of me
making me addicted to his pain.

I lost my willingness
when he submerged my head
in his whites and blues,
and all his hurting.

**—not again.**

hit me
thunders
light and stones,
take me
blow me out.

make of me
fractured quartz on the floor,
start a fire underneath my chin,
all my leaves bathe in mirrors
I closed my eyes and I felt your arms.

you are here to watch me disappear.

**—I can't let you back in.**

my clothes are clean
the dirt has been washed away,
now my grass is as green
as it should have always been.
the notes are rising to the sky
reaching out to the crescent moon
doomed with my suffering
from the drops of venom
going through my blood.
waning moon looking for my soul
to end the curse breathing in my core.
don't forget about the love that started it all.

\-\-**freedom.**

I too had the chance to destroy
every single particle
in the words you shouted,
in your body
in your existence
in your lies
in your weak sex
and short sentences.

I loved you enough not to do so,
I loved myself enough not to do so.

**—stop calling.**

the wolves will come
to consume the powerless warrior
inside of you.
say all the prayers you know,
let me watch how the heavens will ignore
your screaming mouth
like you ignored my dying body
when you stole all my diamonds.

—**honey.**

my heart is a dark hole
swallowing my thoughts
and burning the feelings inside of me,
they scream for salvation
they crave the safety of your arms.

I cannot give myself to you,
still I fall to pieces
on your warm chest.

love me,
love me hard
because I cannot stay.

and I won't.

**—scared of loving.**

I wrote the signs all over your palace,
my blood does not run fast
when I hear your voice
calling for me.
your eyes should have seen
your mind should have read.

the stone you planted in me
is growing,
quit looking for doors,
you cannot stand inside my echoes
shouting to your windows.

—**tasteless.**

falling hearts on mountains peaks,
two melodies being played
by the universe's red hairs.
horses coming down to catch
their souls before they become dust.

sealed together
sacred as the moon
they sing about tears and pilgrims
who bleed through their shields.

they were not meant to be.

**—our truth.**

the flowers you grew with me
are nowhere to be seen,
I'll stand in the grass
holding the ashes of what we were
to watch it all, fall.

these feelings you planted in me
died like seeds on dry grounds.

burn,
burn like fire.
scream.

—**blank.**

I saw it from the back of my head,
all my spine could feel the wheels
coming down
breaking roads
my existence and soul,
leaving blood prints.

something in the ghostly veils
hid the truth with saints and old clothes.
I signed my words with sweat and tears.

but I felt it
and it kept me away.

**—heart.**

I'll break their hearts,
blend their bones
with stones and pieces of shattered glass.
I've fallen too deep into this cave.

they will fall apart
they will cry.

absorbing all the damage
caused by unloving arms that once held me.

**—what did you do.**

every lie coming out of my mouth
is the same coming out of his.
he will never know the weakness of my words
spelling every single one
with thin yet strong lines.

my chest cannot stop the chemicals
disintegrating all my truths.

**—he thought I didn't know.**

she is a silver queen covered in pearls,
holy in her form
graceful like a porcelain doll,
she is the oracle of the moon blessed by God.

pray to the heavens
hoping you'll get help from above
while the sky falls to the ground,
fear takes over your body.

you can't change the shape of a storm,
just like you can't change the soldier in me.

**—I won't change for you.**

after you made me fall asleep
on your breathing chest,
next to all your lies
my thoughts turn to monsters
and all our bricks will remain still
to feel the grounds,
burn.

**—I'm gone.**

the hate you carry
inside your ribs
is eating away your limbs,
soon you'll become the broken dream
from the land of the bitter ones.

you will be remembered as no one's hero,
six feet under
the loneliness and emptiness
surround your fate
for your grave became a cursed cave.

**—I never understood why you hated others so much.**

the scratch cards I kept scratching
were like the boys I kept kissing
that found my lips to be a fountain
to their thirsty mouths.

innocently hoping to find
the one that would hold my hand at night
while my heart was hidden
on a bathroom floor,
crying,
destroyed.

**—lovers, whatever.**

all the nights
with your body next to mine,
after hearing your mouth
vomiting words in the form of weapons,
holding them against my skin,

I still want to hold you.

**—ordrarge.**

hear the beating drums
hitting notes with their own pulse,
standing
in a red room with blood in every inch of me,
shadows
staring at your lifeless body
my hands
holding the knife.
I'll set the house on fire,
there is no knight worth the armor
brewed by injuries and bruises you'd leave on my skin
every night I didn't do what you pleased.

my throat couldn't scream,
my muscles wouldn't move.
I took your soul.

—#14.

here it comes,

quietly in the middle of the night
when nobody can hear a single sound.
the thunder and lightning will cover your voice
while you whisper to my ear,
be careful not to make much noise
you don't want to wake them up.

your shadow crawling up the walls
and your claws
ripping my bed sheets.

the fear is building up inside
and I don't want to close my eyes
I'm scared if I do

I will fall.

**—monster.**

shut the door of my room
I'm hoping for the day
to be over soon,
counting down the hours
minutes
seconds.
I know this is bad,
I don't care.

—**waiting.**

every night
I escape the same trap
every night
I handle the demons coming from behind,
trick the devil
into thinking he's not scary.

sweating
not listening to the words
my pillows are yelling,
the mattress
swallowing my body,
the hands
are choking me.

but you are not so eerie in the morning
and I heard
the sun is coming.

**—sleep in silence.**

my wicked sins
have marked my blood,
there is no need to run
not anymore.

you can't take my soul
for I am one of you,
watch my love slowly burn
all the good is gone.

—**shadows.**

stuck between two walls
coming closer
suffocating me.

when I'm awake
the voices mess with my head,
when I'm asleep
the demons show up in my dreams.

        **—help me.**

all my chromosomes left the roses
I planted in my heart's backyard,
ever since I can't seem to stop moving
swinging back and forth
with my soul wanting to explode.

the flowers are now grey,
emotions strayed
meaningless colors,
I can't bathe in rejoice.

**—give me back my colors.**

the beating muscle in my chest
is only a machine pumping blood
to my veins.

not a heart
not a rose
not a pulse provider.

just a bag filled with air.

—**dark.**

pigments of my blood
everywhere,
all the shades of red on the walls
the pictures stare
at my body alone,
faith shreds
the angels mourn,
my soul is gone.

**—about my aunt, who didn't deserve this.**

big heavy boots on my feet,
the soles are worn
I can feel the stones in every step I take.

the ruins I once called home
do not welcome me anymore,
I'm running away from all the takers,
from all the chain makers.

—**escape.**

they put a crown made of thorns
on my head and tied my hands,
I couldn't move.
they threw me into the den with the lions,
put tape on my lips
so my voice wouldn't be heard.
the sticks and stones hitting my bones
every day
my feet are on a battlefield
every day
my soul is wearing a fake armor made of steel
to fight enemies, I wish I didn't have.

I didn't ask for this,
get me out.

**—high school memories.**

I'm feeling the emptiness on my chest
it's getting harder to breathe,
I know
my nerves soon will shake
my head will scream,

let me out
of this cage you put me in.

                          **—beloved anxiety.**

same old pavements,
barefoot
on pieces of broken roads.
all I see are dead ghosts
and the ruins of old trains
that fell out of space.

I am lost.

**—every day.**

my heart is beating slow,
lying on the ground
under the storm,
the clap of thunder
will take my soul,
tears will fall.
nobody
heard
my
voice.

**—I'm not okay.**

God blessed you with the power
of growing flowers in your garden,
all you did was water the seeds
with liquid touched by the devil,
turning all hopes to ashes
destroying the blossoms with your lies.
our hearts crashed against the walls
you built during our sleep.

sitting on a pedestal like the king
you pretended to be,
when you hit the ground
your finger pointed at me
accusing me of all your hurting.

**—dad.**

watch me hold my breath,
I don't want you here
don't kiss me goodnight.

my grounds will shake again
the spiders will come for me
the night will take over my body
bleeding the poison, the trees will drink
ignoring the warnings
and then,
and then they will blame it on me.

**—let me save you from myself.**

hear the marching band
playing at my funeral,
kiss me on the forehead
do the things you never did
say the words you never said.

you're the only one wearing black
you're the only one who cries.

**—why didn't you help me when I asked for help?**

chains around my limbs
tying a knot around my brain,
repetitive circles around me
choking my sanity.
infected arms from the ground
wanting to grab my feet
to make me stay
and drink the blood in my veins.

this place is deceiving
the silhouettes move
whispering the lies
my mind end up believing.

my God,
please
get these thoughts out of my head.

**—anxious routine.**

I can breathe
feel
hear
speak
fear.

human pieces in me
yet I feel like a broken machine
that cannot be fixed,
and that's all I'll ever be.

**—functioning.**

diving into the black waters
of my soul
counting all the ghosts that have drown,
see the devil in front of me,
hold my tongue.
make the blood rain,
the bodies from hell will drain

MAKE IT RAIN

I'm the only master of my sins
I'll take the blame,
try to burn me with your flames
send the monsters
from the deep dark holes on earth,
bring the demons
their heads will look pretty
as they float on the river.

scream,
it's driving you insane
you can't make me shiver.

**—non metuis.**

the moments when I'm at peace
when the voices have been silent
when my dreams don't become nightmares
and my demons are quiet,

I feel half empty,
is this too bad?

**—this is the only life I've known.**

I can't break the silence trapped in vessels,
there isn't enough blood
in my body to move my fingers
and reach the broken glass on the ground
to cut the ropes holding me down.

I want to scream,
but there isn't a voice in me.

**—drops of loneliness.**

raging storms in my fingers
fighting one another,
my eyes stopped flickering
the violence is in every fiber
every bone
every stone thrown at me.

I've counted all the freckles
on my mother's body
every wrinkle on her toes,
all the hairs in her head.

uncontrollably burning
flash fire on my chest,
I can keep counting
but it won't stop from taking over
my whole existence.

—**anger.**

I can feel your intentions
coming out of your pores
in sweat form
building up the tension,
running to the storm.

stay there.

don't get too close,
you'll be standing in gore.

**—what I've become.**

yellow teeth in the mirror
red marks on my skin
shattered lips go with my broken nails,
an unloved object.

my reflection is a monster,
I am one too
we are both irrelevant.

**—reality.**

home,
where the tears meet
the need to stop my breathing,
a place that has seen the worst of me
but it doesn't close the doors
or the windows.
instead it opens the curtains
letting the light hit my face.

the place that stops me from sobbing
from hurting
from craving poison,
it has felt my screaming
it has seen me get lost in four walls
lose my voice,
my strength.

it doesn't crumble or shake,
it holds me tight
it doesn't stop loving me.

—**someone.**

the best lies are the ones
you create to protect yourself
from a mountain waiting to collapse,
ready to bury you.

**—when I say I'm okay.**

just let me go
let me burn
let me be alone.

I don't know what to do
without having you
staring at my darkness.

let me hide,
let me die.

**—losing lovers.**

all of me has been drained
the rain
won't stop falling
won't stop filling my room with its water.

soon
I'll be drowning.

**—tiredness.**

should I take my heart out of my chest,
let it feel its nerves shaking
as the ground breaks
from the earthquake that is causing
my emotional wreck?

no.

**—scared of loving.**

my room hides the illusion
of wolves howling
hungry for blood.
I will pray for them to rip me apart.

for my spirit is gone,
can't move the rocks on my back,
I need to close my eyes.

**—exhausted.**

I am the murderer
and the murdered,
trapped in a cage.

they come
they get close
my eyes restrain
my hands resist
from taking their key.

I am the slaughter
and the slaughtered,
the emptiness of my heart
is reaching to my brain,

I am inside the cage,
they are here to stare.

**—social anxiety.**

dark shadows
under night lights
wandering the streets
coming after me,
I count every step they take
I am aware of every move they make.
night terrors
awake the fear in me.
I wonder how many lives I have left.

    **—walking home at night.**

I saw the trees grow
and now they just burn.
all the houses I built with my hands
turn to ashes,
I feel the knives cutting my face
as the air gets darker.

everything falls off my shoulders
and I hear it breaking.

**—still lost.**

my roots are too deep to get loose,
my white colored sins are the white noise
going through my ears.

I've lost everything,
the birds don't sing my way
I've smothered myself.

—**strong.**

the places I left behind
hold my past as a prisoner,
my skin turns red
the sun is far from being warm.
hold the gun against my head,
I'm wandering a desert in my mind.

**—help me disappear.**

the more I breathe
the deeper I drown.

castles stumble behind
the river of demons pulling out the cement
little by little.

**—days.**

the marks throughout my spine won't disappear.
I can't look at myself in the mirror,
the lines on my arms
can be tracked down
to a grey past where the clouds
would let the rain fall
over my wounds
making it hard to stay alive.

the plants in my garden won't grow.

**—listen to me, please.**

if I could put all my life in a photograph,
hold it in my hands
wash away the stains that made my heart bleed,
paint the old lovers black and white,
mark the places on my body
where his hands have been,
show the bruises that still hurt.

put it all on paper for me to keep,
to hold close to my heart,
buried in my skin
help the memories find a new pulse.

I wouldn't,
it's not worth it.

**—I only want to forget.**

they are getting closer
I hear the fear rumbling in my veins.
the monsters are coming
they will hunt me down
burn my flesh
steal my soul,
dragging me to hell
but I need to stay.

**—fighting my depression.**

the days I don't feel like writing
are the days I feel the most scared of,
I can't let my mind wander.

if I do
the voices will start talking
my body will start shaking
my leg won't stop moving,
they will win
they will take over.

**—I can't let the voices win.**

don't let me drown in the past,
all the nights I've been praying
I'm begging to believe
my wounds will heal.
you're all I have,
I don't trust myself,
don't lock the door.

my voice is breaking,
I don't want to lay on my bed
to watch the bed sheets turn red.

> **—I know I failed but I need your help.**

virginity,
overrated
fragile little thing.
I felt dirty
like it had been my fault again.
I had to lie to that woman's face
to protect myself
from her judgmental eyes.

**—but I am a survivor.**

let me run,
I'm falling deep into the sea
of lies and ties made of thorns
don't hold my hand,
there are monsters hiding under the mattress
getting drunk with the venom.

I hid my soul in the woods,
but let me hide behind the warm sun,
let me pretend.

> **—maybe I just feel okay for a second.**

it's hard to breathe
my lungs cannot find the air,
my mind cannot cease
the nuclear war inside my head.

I'm sinking
drowning in my own poison.

—**survive.**

in my head lies are hiding
behind the damaged jars the beasts
put in my hands,
I am waiting for all the colors
to go from yellow to grey.

my willingness to live has gone extinct,
dark shadows and shapes
whispering to my windows,

my doors are closed.

—**bad week.**

no matter how many times I fall on the ground
how many times the voices win
and drag me down to the toxic cave
where depression hides
and the hands of anxiety tie my arms.

I want someone who will love me through it,
not save me
just love me.

—**I want.**

death I forgive you
for taking my diamonds,
for hiding the spark in their eyes.
please
put me in a place
where I can see all the remains
of the love I have given,
where I can see their faces
on a vibrant summer night.

**—the ones I've lost.**

I lost my mind long ago
when the mountain collapsed in my eyes
splitting every thought in two,
creating echoes
awakening monsters
ghosts whispering words I wish I couldn't hear,
when a river of blood ruined the fire
and made it all dark.

**—9 years ago.**

my lips, so dry they are cracked
the sun
burning my skin
now as red as the blood running in my veins.
heavy air
heavy thoughts.

I'm starting to drift,
slowly disappearing.

       **—it's winning.**

pretty face
perfect teeth
take a bite off of me.
my soul won't join the cult
kill me
murder me
cover me with gasoline
light me up.

**—can't fit in your world.**

I'm trying really hard
to paint a good picture
of your heart.

all the times you hit my body
like it was a punching bag
are holding my brushes captive.

**—house.**

the sunset is sinking in,
low bass sounds hit my brain
like birds singing,
I will not survive the fate
of my oceans drying.

my hands are tied up,
kill me
I don't want to see
I don't want to breathe
or hear.

kill me in the morning
or after the sun sets.
I want to find the place
where my sins will collapse.

**—it went wrong.**

I lost count of all the lies I've said to you,
I only wanted to keep you safe
from the monsters living inside of me.
I am an imposter
and I wanted to cover your eyes
so you couldn't see the vultures
flying around waiting for you
to lay on the ground and fall asleep
to pick your eyes out.

I know you wouldn't hear my voice
and I know you wouldn't look at me
the same way you used to
before you knew.

  **—hiding my c-ptsd from my boyfriends.**

I'd move all the mountains
swim through all the oceans
to hold on close to your existence,
but I had to hide my emotions
from all the thunder
your anger was causing.

**—not about a lover.**

they hid under beds
whispering how they'd take
all that was left of your bravery,
every monster in your head,
unsweetened crawling
with cracked nails
built under nightmares,
they never wanted anything from you
except all your happiness.

**—friends.**

keep it.
keep my heart
my thoughts,
my chromosomes,
my soul
my eyes
my hair
my bones.

I do not want
I do not need
any of these things.

**—feeling like nothing.**

I want to stay in the clouds
above the rain
where I'm safe.
but my feet had never wandered
around those places.

   **—where is my peace of mind?**

my spirit is feeling incomplete
unworthy.
in the distance I see
my dying body,
lungs lacking oxygen.

I don't mind.

**—depression.**

let me stay beside your bed,
where the monsters came to bury you again,

so that we can die
and feel our beating hearts
be consumed by the fire.

**—from me, to me.**

maybe I should let you know
there's a shadow on my shoulders,
within the sunlight
between the trees
hanging on my neck,
over my soul.

it's made of fire,
despair,
agony
and tears.

**—bruises.**

my ribs are tied,
my soul is yet to be purified.
my body is unholy.

I'll walk the seven seas
for you to set me free,
my spirit is tired,
my heart is aching
stopping its beats.

make the waves take my sorrow,
the tidal forces
break the ropes keeping me from finding peace.

I have sinned
my vessel is unclean,
save me
from this misery.

**—conscientiam.**

take this moment,
take it from its roots
grab it by the horns
like a bull coming up to you
ready to eat you whole
while you still breathe.

you can win this battle,
do not give up,
you can build a castle with its bones.

**—thoughts I try to keep during panic attacks.**

there is fire in your eyes.
you carry the strength of a dragon
your presence is intimidating
like an army of ten thousand warriors.

**—reminder.**

I want you to let me in,
I want to hold your hand.
put your armor down,
let me break the shield
around your heart.

**—let me love you.**

forgive me,
for drowning in an empty ocean
for being afraid of the storm.

countless nights
spent swimming in regret
hiding from your arms.
you fixed me
when I was broken.
saved me
from my thoughts
falling off the edge
when they weren't holding on
to your grace.

you stayed,
you never left.

**—I was mad at you and I'm sorry.**

there's a tree outside my window,
I know it's silly
but I think I fell in love with it.

the way it moves
reminds me of you.
the leaves fall in time,
it puts them behind
like you did with all your fears
in the past.

I see the tree every day,
it's so close
yet so far from my touch.
I see it swing with the wind
flirt with the birds
making me wish I had wings.

this tree,
reminds me of us.
so close,
yet so far away.

**—the dancing tree outside my window.**

close the door
fill the room with our love.
suck the blood on my neck
let me grasp you with my nails
kiss my body
kiss my lips
kiss me
I never want to forget.

**—route 32.**

lay here
with me
look me in the eye
get lost in my hands,
forget about time
watch our colors blend
while the pain
fades away.
it's just you and I,
we can start
all over again.

                    **—hold my hand one more time.**

your words,
have never been so strong
you,
have never sounded so sure
telling me you need me
telling me
you want me close.

**—I wish you could decide.**

let me take you by the hand
wipe your tears,
I'll save you from the monsters
from the restless chase
from the shadows coming closer.

let me take you to the unknown land
where the beasts will be your friends,
the roses will talk and the sun will shine.

I promise,
I will not let you get lost in the dark
I'll put you in my heart
until you can find some peace of mind.

I'll keep you there,
safe and sound.

    **—things I wish my lover said to me.**

I found my life
when I looked into your eyes
I found the stars
when I was falling apart.
blood,
still running through my veins.
the air
caressing my face.

you showed me the universe
with the loving words coming out of your mouth.

  **—I found the universe in your eyes.**

this is my place to be,
around your arms.
your voice
singing to my ear
is my melody,
you set me free.

the ocean waves
making love to the sea.
this is our fate.

—**wild.**

when you held my hand
I wanted to run away with you,
find a new place
we could call home.
I wanted to kiss your lips
get lost in your arms
feel all the chemicals in my body exploding
as the walls in my heart
start to fall and the doors open
to welcome you.

**—what our first kiss felt like.**

give me a bottle
to drink your poison,
pour it on my body
and watch it run free on my skin,
every drop on me.
make me shine with the oils
in your fingers
like a river running wild
under the sunlight.

**—in the afternoon.**

she will dance with the wind
spinning around
wearing a yellow dress that glows
with the light from the sun.

her smile was like warm blankets
on a rainy day
making you feel so calm.
she makes all the dark
colors disappear.
bringing the bright ones
blending them with her hands
to put them all over your face.

everything is okay
when she's here.
she's a dandelion girl.

**—flowers in my head.**

don't close the windows
the air will get stuck,
don't open your mouth
to spit words with a broken tongue.

all the heavy wounds will open up and heal,
place the stitches on the red skin
my love for you is growing stronger
with your wings up in my head,
my voice will sing.

**—reach out.**

I am worthy of love,
I am more than sad poems
broken hearts
horrible monsters,
I am more than just a body.

I am good enough.

**—reaffirmations in the morning.**

mother,
the most beautiful
diamond
on earth you are.
let me keep you safe,
feed you,
guide your steps.

—**forgiveness.**

in the shadows
where all my hope is broken
he will come
to rescue my soul,
his hands
so soft
handling my mistakes,
raising me from the ground.
creating light
with my darkness.

—**castles.**

you and I,
two infinite lines
swirling, touching, fading away
then finding each other again,
stuck in a magnetic field
waiting to collapse.

we are ethereal,
I love it as much as I love you.

**—june 9th.**

we are planes,
falling into our gravity.
melting
into the infinity,
like two galaxies
colliding.

        **—beautiful.**

I fell in love with your art,
your dark brown beard
your hands
your dreams.

the grey days wouldn't be blue
when we hid in rooms
during cold nights
to make them warm.

        **—every week.**

I keep making the same mistakes.

ignoring you knocking on my door,
placing your delicate hands on my heart,
bringing me peace
wrapping me in your light.

I still make storms out of broken floors
and burned out walls.

you still love me.

**—stubborn.**

tell me
how I ended up swimming
in your haunted ocean?
how am I not drowning?

why am I floating like a boat
in the summer?
you messed me up
by building up a smile with my mouth.
now I am stuck
pouring all my feelings
on swinging pearls.

—**amor.**

spellbinding prismatic moth
in the night sky,
singing curses with my wings.
the queen of Neptune you say I am,
rare as a fire-plated coin.

**—queen of Neptune.**

give me ten thousand nights with you,
to caress the gold in your blood,
breathe the same air
take the same steps,
throw you into my lake
while I sit and watch your naked body swim.

**—her.**

the night is cold
my feet are stuck in a frozen river,
slowly losing all my senses.
I see it coming for me
moving like a hurricane.

cannot be stopped.
but you are here.

**—this time I'm not scared.**

heavy weather

you make me feel like flowers
sunbathing
and two trains
crashing.

**—finding love.**

the waves will sing to me
all the love songs
I want to hear,
I will give my scarlet lips to you,
I'll get drunk in your waters
becoming one with your currents.

seduce me with your deep blue soul
so I can kiss a piece
of the memories that are now a blur.
sing to me
all the love songs you know.
it's only you and I after all.

**—soledad.**

when you are here
all my fears fade away in pieces,
open my veins and eyes
heal my wounds.
your presence is all I need,
light up a candle that will never run out
I can hear angels sing,
wrap me up in your love blankets.

**—fearless.**

the blue marks you'd leave on my neck,
were my favorite work of art.
your lips,
touching mine,
my favorite way to die.

**—today, I missed you.**

all of me is tired,
my body can't get any rest.
hold me in your arms
take me to your house
cover me with your bed sheets,
sing me to sleep
fix me with your kisses.

love me,
love my demons.

**—instructions.**

you are the water
I needed,
you are the earth
I was searching.
you are the sun
I am a rose,
you are making me bloom.

**—I'm yours.**

I am just a shattered glass
almost six feet under.
my thoughts,
burying me down
not good enough
for the light,
so pure.

majestic bright love,
I can hear the sounds
I can feel
the wind lifting me up,
a healing melody.

my soul,
bathed in gold.

**—before and after.**

the beauty of his lips,
his sun kissed skin
could only be found on my dreams,
in my fingers tracing paths on him
during his sleep.

**—perfection.**

make me pure again,
clean my skin
wash away all the sins
with your loving hands.

your holy ghost
will follow me
for the rest of my existence.
making me feel
sacred vibrations.

**—midnight wonders.**

I found love in your arms
when all of me was shaking,
when I was pushing you away
my hands hitting your chest,
my soul and spirit fighting
to stay in my body.

you held me close,
when my demons tried to devour me.

—**first time.**

come
hold me close
hold my thoughts,
discover the lands my love hides.
my heart forgot how to feel
but my veins,
my veins create storms inside
of me with my blood
every time my eyes
stumble upon you.

**—for you, when you said you felt sad.**

the most beautiful sound I've ever heard,
you
drowning in my love,
hopelessly falling,
trusting my hands are there to catch you.

**—they are there.**

I am scared of the ocean.
I wanted to run away
from the waves,
your love kept me here
now my feet
no longer touch the sand
but your hands
are holding me tight.

I am willing to wander
unknown currents
as long as I am with you.

**—lead my feet.**

covered by your love
bringing life to my core,
giving strength to my bones.
like an avalanche
getting rid of my old roots,
your eyes
help me move and show me the truth
as the sound waves go through my body
healing my spirit
picking up the pieces
putting them back together.

with your love,
all the pain is gone
and my lungs can breathe again.

—**Hosanna.**

I get lost in bright mirrors
promising to become diamonds,
getting closer I see
they are burned carbon.

forgiveness will come to me
in my dark room,
the bricks built a wall around my feet,
I will fall asleep on my regrets.
I know my heart won't stop trying to betray me
but his love will find me,
his love will save me.

**—I shouldn't wander outside my home.**

fire burning through my veins
and spikes ripping up my skin are all I know,
but one by one
my scars disappear.
one by one
my wounds start to forget
when the pain would hold my hopes
tying them to black holes.

my eyes could not see.

you,
your tender love,
is giving me salvation.

**—speak to me.**

in your arms I want to rest
my legs are weak and I cannot stand,
give me strength to walk
under the rain that's wearing me out
give me a heart to fight,
take me with you
take me to places I never knew.

take me,
just take me
love me
save me.

                                                **—nothing compares.**

be still in my heart.
don't move.
you're the only one who will hold my ground
when my thoughts start a raging war,
and screams of all the voices in the past
get to my ears.

—**#5.**

I found you
sleeping under a tree
looking calm and precious,
I fell asleep next to you
so we could share the dream.

**—it's you.**

your pulse will teach me how to move,
in your eyes I see the desire
waiting to devour me.
I'll let your fingers do the tricks
underneath the bed sheets,
take me to the wonders of your mind.

lose control,
hold on to your favorite parts of my body,
your loving
will never be too much,
move your hands to the rhythm of your heartbeat,
do it one more time
then do it all over again.

—**courage.**

I'll find a burning star
place it in your hands,
I promise you
it will be so bright
you'll put it inside your cold heart
and it will melt into diamonds.

**—the real you.**

she is the bravest horse,
burning brighter than fire
the strongest soldier,
her shield is made of wounds
heavier than all the stars in the universe.

**—she is my mother.**

my knees were tired of fighting
against the burning dirt.
my feet,
could not hold the weight of my muscles and bones.
save my heart at night
keep me close in the morning.
your voice
all I need,
I put my life in your hands
I know you will heal all my scars,
write your name in my heart with threads made of gold.

**—I know you are here.**

he made the broken bones in my stomach
become beautiful butterflies
shining as bright as the sun,
he breathes into my lungs.

how have I been surviving
without his light in my life?

**—thank you for being you.**

when you are in front of me
I see all the colors.
bright blues, pastel greens,
every possible hue.
I am addicted to you,
to your rainbow colored blood.

**—love me in purple.**

my silenced throat
has been restored by you.
the one who created the moon
took my heart
to fix it when it broke,
sealing it with his grace.

**—you.**

my lense will capture your spirit
in your darkest days
when you don't want to see
the colors pouring from your skin,
the flowers in your head,
the diamonds in your eyes.

                        **—you're beautiful mom.**

heavens found me in pieces
while my feet wandered away from home.
lost,
blindfolded,
stumbled upon your feet
with tears falling off my chin.
your voice picked me up.

the cross,
my redemption.

**—from dust.**

I will pour roses on your body,
diamonds on your chest.

Ignoring all the words your tongue spits,
all the words you don't mean to say.

**—sun.**

the birds are singing
and the flowers are blooming.
my mind is falling
for all the pigments of your essence,
my heart is beating faster
pumping blood to my veins,
rising the temperature,
my hands are no longer shaking.

you are my angel.

**—falling in love.**

your emerald eyes and pearly skin,
delicate hands
showing all the years
you've fought to thrive.
wrinkles on your face
hold on to the wisdom of your age,
like a secret they need to keep safe.

the beauty of your heart
is something worth admiring,
you are the queen
of the land you have tilled.
my ears cannot get tired
of listening you speak
the words you kept hidden
between your fingers
and nails.

—**grandma.**

in your eyes
between the sparks,
your fears hide
holding your hands,
old chains wrapping your wrists
hurting your scars
infecting your thoughts
and grabbing your throat.

let me set you free.

**—fear of loving me.**

nothing is bigger than your love,
your patience
your compassion,
nothing is more infinite
than your eternity.
I am yours,
forever.

—**abba.**

my heart,
it is locked and trapped
under a million stones,
it is shattered
it became a puzzle with missing parts.

still,
do not let my heart
make you doubt,
do not let my heart
make your hands sweat and your whole body shake,
do not let my heart
inject you with its fear of failure.
do not let it.

**—you're enough.**

I was listening to the waves
as they carried away
the defeated heads of my long lost warriors.
I kept fighting,
praying to the heavens
begging
for it to calm the heavy weather.
hoping to restore my destroyed faith
to change my fate.

—**pray.**

inside,
under all my layers,
I keep you hidden.
don't want anyone to see
don't want anyone to touch.
your words consume me like fire
burning during the night.

I'll come running,
until my feet become dust.
one day we will float away
on a solid surface.

**—on but sometimes off.**

heart,
listening to the sounds
the shimmering voices sing
after crushing splinters came in waves
leaving only broken glass
on dirty grounds.
start to feel
don't skip beats,
find joy in this love.
a love higher than the mountains,
as bright as the moon in the dark.

**—healing.**

I will be found praying
when my body is shaking
in fear of all the battles to come.
I will call out His name
to save me from hell,
to save me from myself.

the stones tied to feet are heavy.

**—trust.**

raise our voices
until they are heard,
put rocks in our way
you can kill our bodies
you can't take our will.
destroy what you see
our conviction will stand,
our spirits will not break
you
will never forget our names.

            **—women.**

twisted tongues
darker lies,
carrying broken limbs and dirty clothes
from when I let go of his hand.

open the heavens
pour them in my oceans.

I am not afraid of my demons
trying to devour me.

—**update.**

sometimes I fear,
standing in front of the abyss
I hear all the voices screaming.
I fear,
I fear you turn your face away from me
I fear you take your love
and hide it from my heart,
from a heart that craves
your diamond waters,
your eyes caressing my soul,
from a heart that craves you.

**—fear of losing.**

I want to have you in my room,
I want to read your soul
and kiss your ear lying on my neck,
let me call your name
in the snow while my thoughts freeze
and create a war inside my head,
so I can put you under my river
and keep you there.
forever.

—**hostage.**

under a december night
you stood next to me
putting your arm on hips,
making me swing with the lights
and beats of all the hearts
that were sweating and shining bright.
I saw your freckles
as you held and kissed my hand.

**—I will never forget about you.**

the ray of light coming from you
can break the darkest patterns
build castles
create cold fire
and stop me from crying.

**—maybe it's love.**

because of all the times I've craved your love
you never came running,
not once.
not ever.

yet my heart cannot stop melting
to the sound of your voice
and the brightness of your smile.
I can hear the horses coming
crawling from the deep ends
of the burning
undying jar
with exploding glass,
stabbing my heart.

I'll die.

         **—always his.**

all my blood runs freely
but I know you'll catch it in your hands
and all the honey that's filling
my head has got a safe place to stay.

I never thought you'd light me up this way,
I never thought you'd be the one I'd call home.

my lungs were a burning forest,
your mouth,
a river going through my veins ceasing the fire
making the flowers growing in my chest
shine bright and not fall apart
like little nothings shattering on the ground.

**—falling in love with the right person.**

I don't want to make
the most fragile nerves
in your body vibrate like guitar strings.

not tonight.

I want to hear you speak.

remember what your voice sounded like
the joy it would bring to my ears.
I want to see you throwing up the diamonds
you kept for yourself all this time.

I want to hear you say
you love me.

**—the last time.**

the love I craved, was found in your arms.
your existence is strong like thunder,
light me up with your fire.
I want to take your purple kiss
all over my skin,
burn all my past with your desire.

you can witness all my weaknesses,
drink up all my tension and still be mine.

**—this is how I know you're real.**

on a rainy day
you held my hand,
grabbed my hips like I was yours,
like you were mine.

your eyes lit up
when your lips caressed
what was left of me.

                **—my first kiss under the rain.**

in the morning when the birds sing
we found our hands intertwined,
close your eyes
feel our lungs breathe as one.
my spirit will love you,
so will I.

stay,
I will too.

**—unexpected.**

all my heartbeats start to shiver
as my world is blending with yours
and my hands build a castle with your lips.
your light and darkness live in my dreams,
my broken colors melt again
to the sound of your touch.

my time is consumed
by your burgundy colored essence,
I love to feel the air
filling my body to write your name
under my skin.

**—your favorite color.**

bathing in water from stones,
the doors are closing in my head
and my windows will not open,
the air,
is getting heavy like thunder
falling on pieces of my broken hope.

help me catch your breath,
get me out of this state.
your hands are the feathers
my heart needs to feel.

**—a billion times.**

a thousand times I heard your voice
guiding my eyes to your face,
but the crushing waves called my name.
I feel into a never-ending cave with ghosts
gripping my skin,
demons pulling my hair,
but you carried my beaten body
putting me into the safety of your hands.

I do not vomit dead flowers since then.

**—from dirt.**

your hand reaching out to me
to save my life every time
the shaky grounds fall apart,
pouring rain from the heavens,
water drops falling on broken vessels.

bring your love to my heart
hear my prayers
screaming like the earth going dry,
send a chariot made of fire,
save me.

**—miles and miles.**

in darkness you will hold me,
the depths won't fall on my shoulders,
night terrors won't come for me
the grounds do not shake with the steps
of the heavy soles from my past.

no need to hold my breath.
I can see your shape
standing strong in front of my face.

—**protector.**

his truths have broken all my lies
all my ties and chains.
I see his heart leading my feet
making me walk,
feeling alive.
erasing all my failures.
like sweet chords to my ears he is.

**—hug me.**

I'm a broken bottle
something lost,
abandoned.
but I belong to you,
I belong in your eyes,
in your green pearls and colored skies.

**—learning.**

forever I will hold on to your promise
of everlasting love.
when my grounds break
I know I will be safe
for I have found a shelter in your heart.

I will never be forsaken.

**—I love you more now.**

I come from a billion years
submitted to hundred billion sins,
a thousand battles I had to survive.

I won every single one.
I was not alone,
never was.

                                      **—he was with me.**

release all your loving essence
singing forever about your love,
all of you in my blood.
make oceans out of me
waves from my tears,
deeper than the dark waters
stronger than lightning hitting on shadows.
your love keeps me alive,
give me life
give me earth.

→ **—remain.**

it is amazing to feel
the fresh breeze on my skin.

so liberating.

**—happiness.**

your love begins in forgotten places
and my prism awakens
whenever you speak.
insecurities unfold as my mask
falls to hit the floors.

I would never run away,
I would never reject
your loving grace.

**—I'm glad you found me.**

in the darkness your light will guide my way,
your breath will lift me.
make your stars burn during the dark in me
as your love rests on my face.

you revive all my hopes
all my flames,
all my strength.

—**mercy.**

let your love come through me,
your wild rivers clean my spirit,
all my feelings
consumed by the chemicals.
my heart surrenders
as I fall to your feathers.

my skin loves to feel your loving sun on me,
the rain falls over my body
to mark a new beginning.

**—you save me.**

when I close my eyes
you're all I see,
you're in my deepest thoughts
in my darkest clouds
in my brightest skies.

you're all I want,
my entire existence I want to spend
thinking of you.

**—all I want, all I need.**

You.

**—the reason why I haven't given up.**

thank you for walking with me through every page of this book, for your patience and kindness, for holding my hand, my heart and softly wrapping me in your arms.

thank you, for reading a part of me.

# acknowledgements

Jair Sandoval

Odette Chaves

Arturo Vega

there would be no book without them.

*Heavy Weather* Copyright © 2017 by Ness Lobo.

All rights reserved. No part of this book may be distributed, reproduced or transmitted in any form or by any means without the express written permission except for the use of brief quotations in a book review.

ISBN: 978-0-692-98987-6

@prismaticmoth

www.ingramcontent.com/pod-product-compliance
Lightning Source LLC
Chambersburg PA
CBHW051935290426
44110CB00015B/1989